Nos encantan las ciencias
So Into Science!

EXPLOREMOS
LA CHARCA
EXPLORING THE
THE POND

Marie Roesser
Traducido por / Translated by Eida de la Vega

Gareth Stevens
PUBLISHING

Please visit our website, www.garethstevens.com. For a free color catalog of all our high-quality books, call toll free 1-800-542-2595 or fax 1-877-542-2596.

Library of Congress Cataloging-in-Publication Data

Names: Roesser, Marie, author.
Title: Exploring the pond = Exploremos la charca / Marie Roesser.
Description: New York : Gareth Stevens Publishing, 2019. | Series: So into science! = Nos encantan las ciencias | Includes index.
Identifiers: LCCN 2018013147| ISBN 9781538236345 (library bound)
Subjects: LCSH: Pond ecology–Juvenile literature. | Pond animals–Juvenile literature. | Ponds–Juvenile literature.
Classification: LCC QH541.5.P63 R64 | DDC 577.63/6–dc23
LC record available at https://lccn.loc.gov/2018013147

Published in 2019 by
Gareth Stevens Publishing
111 East 14th Street, Suite 349
New York, NY 10003

Translator: Eida de la Vega
Editor, English: Therese Shea
Designer: Sarah Liddell

Photo credits: Cover, p. 1 Iness Arna/Shutterstock.com; pp. 5, 17 Yuriy Kulik/Shutterstock.com; p. 7 aPhoenixPhotographer/Shutterstock.com; pp. 9, 24 (minnow) Rostislav Stefanek/Shutterstock.com; p. 11 Miroslav Halama/Shutterstock.com; p. 13 optimarc/Shutterstock.com; pp. 15, 24 (crayfish) Geza Farkas/Shutterstock.com; p. 19 vig64/Shutterstock.com; p. 21 Adri Hoogendijk/Buiten-beeld/Minden Pictures/Minden Pictures/Getty Images; p. 23 Dimedrol68/Shutterstock.com.

Printed in the United States of America

CPSIA compliance information: Batch #CW19GS: For further information contact Gareth Stevens, New York, New York at 1-800-542-2595.

Contenido

Contents

La charca es un cuerpo de agua pequeño. ¡Esta es nuestra charca!

A pond is a small body of water. This is our pond!

Las charcas tienen
agua dulce.
No son saladas.

....

Ponds have freshwater.
They aren't salty.

Los foxinos (pececillos)
son peces de charca.
Son pequeños.
¡Nadan rápido!

Minnows are
pond fish.
They are small.
They swim fast!

Los róbalos son peces
de charca.
Son grandes.
¡Comen ranas!

....

Bass are pond fish.
They are big.
They eat frogs!

Las ranas ponen
huevos en la charca.
¡Y de ellos salen
los renacuajos!

Frogs lay eggs
in the pond.
Tadpoles come out!

Los langostinos
viven en la charca.
Ellos comen
renacuajos.

....

Crayfish live
in the pond.
They eat tadpoles!

Alrededor de la charca
crecen hierbas.
Algunas plantas crecen en
el agua. ¡Veo nenúfares!

Grasses grow
around the pond.
Some plants grow in the
water. I see water lilies!

Los patos hacen
nidos en la hierba.
Ellos esconden
sus huevos.

Ducks make nests
in the grass.
They hide their eggs!

Las arañas hacen
telarañas junto
a la charca.
¡Veo un insecto
en la telaraña!

Spiders make webs
by the pond.
I see a bug in the web!

¡Las charcas están llenas de vida!

....

Ponds are full of life!

Palabras que debes aprender
Words to Know

(el) langostino
crayfish

(el) foxino
minnow

Índice / Index